Drip! Drop!

HOW WATER GETS TO YOUR TAP

by Barbara Seuling
illustrated by Nancy Tobin

Featuring: JoJo and her dog, Willy

SCHOLASTIC INC.
New York Toronto London Auckland Sydney
Mexico City New Delhi Hong Kong Buenos Aires

ISBN 0-439-31859-9

Text copyright © 2000 by Barbara Seuling.
Illustrations copyright © 2000 by Nancy Tobin.
All rights reserved.
Published by Scholastic Inc., 555 Broadway, New York, NY 10012,
by arrangement with Holiday House, Inc.
SCHOLASTIC and associated logos are trademarks
and/or registered trademarks of Scholastic Inc.

12 11 10 9 8 7 6 5 4 3   2 3 4 5 6/0

Printed in the U.S.A.   09

First Scholastic printing, October 2001

You turn on the tap.
Drip! Drop!
Cool, clean water comes out.

The sun heats the water
in the oceans and lakes.

The warm water evaporates.
It rises into the air as vapor.

Up in the sky the
water vapor forms clouds.

WATER VAPOR

It's cold up in the sky.

When the water vapor gets really cold, it turns back into water.

Water comes in three forms: a liquid (the way it comes out of the tap), a gas (water vapor), and a solid (ice, which is frozen water).

Then it falls from the clouds
as millions of tiny water drops.

We call this rain or snow.

No matter how much water evaporates,
it always comes back to earth as rain, snow, hail, frost, sleet, or dew.

Only 1 percent of the water on earth,
a teeny-tiny bit, is good to drink.
The rest is salty, as in the oceans, or frozen in glaciers.

Water soaks into the ground.
Streams fill up and flow into rivers.
Rivers flow down mountains
and back to the ocean.

This is the water cycle.

People need water

to drink...

to wash...

and to cook.

They need it to
feed their animals...

to water their gardens...

They pump it up from under the ground.

A person can live only a few days without water.

They wait for rain and catch it.

They go to the river and carry it home.

Big pipes carry water from
the rivers and streams and under
the ground to a reservoir.

A reservoir is a place that holds water. The
water goes from the reservoir to the city.

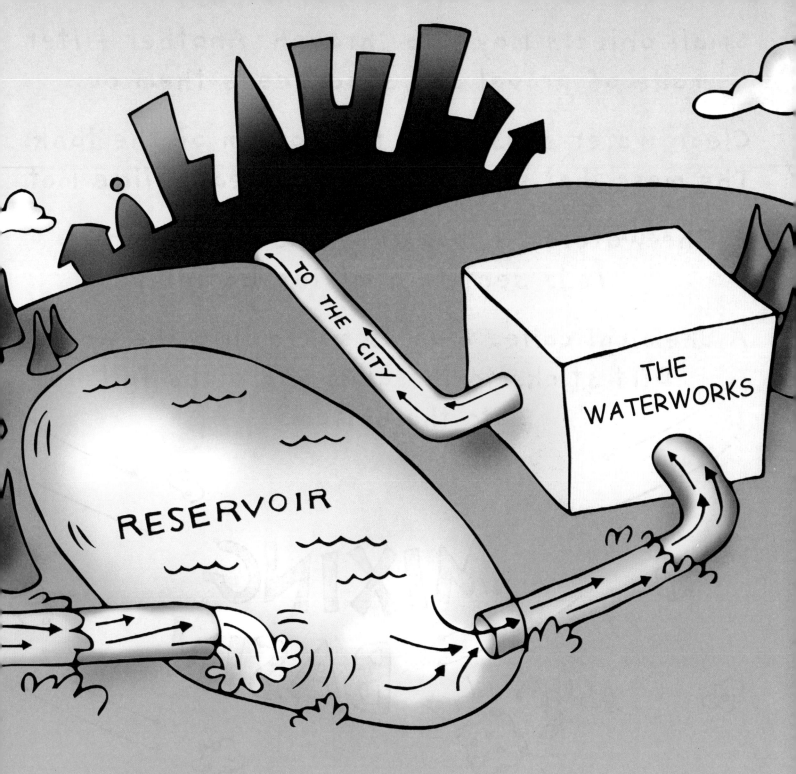

But first, it must be cleaned.

Large objects are filtered out of the water—
fish, feathers, fur, boots, plastic bags, leaves.

Small objects may slip through. Another filter made of gravel and sand keeps them out.

Clean water ends up at the bottom of the tank. The mess that stays on top is called a slime mat.

The water still has tiny bits of dirt in it. It is sent to a mixing basin.

A chemical called alum is mixed into the water. Dirt sticks to the alum and globs fall to the bottom.

MIXING BASIN

ALUM

A drop of water under a microscope.

The water is still
not ready to drink.
There may be bacteria in it.

You can't see bacteria,
but it can make you sick.

There may be minerals
like iron or calcium in the water.
They can make it taste or smell bad.

The water goes to the
water treatment plant
of the waterworks.

Scientists taste the water. They smell it.

They take out minerals, such as sulfur, which smells bad.

They add chemicals, such as chlorine, that kill bacteria.

When the water is clean and safe, it can leave the waterworks.

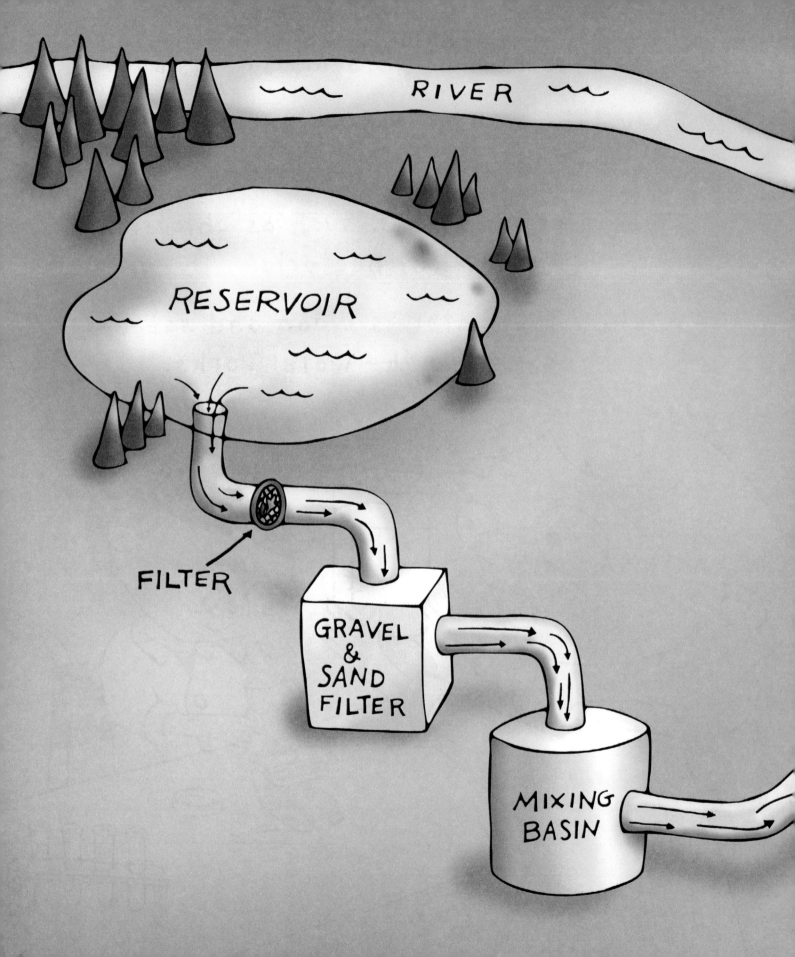

RIVER

RESERVOIR

FILTER

GRAVEL
&
SAND
FILTER

MIXING
BASIN

Water pressure pushes the water up through the walls.

or too fast.

You are thirsty.
A drink of water would be nice.
You turn on the tap. Drip! Drop!
Cool, clean water comes out.

And you know just how it got there!

Dr. JoJo's Science Lab

Make Water EVAPORATE

1 You will need:

 2 plastic containers

 1 lid

 1 glass of water

 a tablespoon

 a sunny place, or lamplight

2 Put 2 tablespoons of water in each container.
Place the lid tightly on one of the containers.

3

Place the containers side by side in a sunny spot or under a lighted lamp. Let the containers sit there all day.

4

The next day, look at the two containers. The container with the lid still has water in it. The open container has no water in it. The warm water rose into the air and became water vapor. It evaporated!

Dr. JoJo's Science Lab

Make Your Own WATER FILTER

① You will need:

☐ 1 glass with water in it

1 empty glass

☐ a strainer

☐ a spoonful of sand or dirt

☐ a coffee filter

☐ a rubber band

☐ 3 small objects, such as a button, a paper clip, and a scrap of paper

② Put the dirt and the objects in the glass of water.

③ Pour the water through the strainer into the empty glass. The objects will stay in the strainer, but the dirt will go through.

④ Rinse the glass that is now empty. Put the coffee filter over it. Hold it on with the rubber band.

⑤ Slowly pour the water through the coffee filter into the empty glass. The filter keeps the remaining dirt from going into the water.

You even have your own slime mat!

Dr. Jo Jo's Science Lab

Make Your Own RAINDROPS

1 You will need:

- [ ] an empty food can
- [ ] water
- [ ] ice
- [ ] food coloring

2 Wash the can and peel off the label.

Dry the outside of the can. Fill it with ice.

3

Add water about halfway up to the top. Add a few drops of food coloring. Let it stand for a few minutes.

4

In a little while the can will look like it's "sweating." Drops of water form on the outside of the can. They are not colored. That means the water is not leaking out of the can!
The air outside the can is cooled by the ice. When water vapor in the air is cold, it changes back into liquid water, and drops form. This is just what happens when water vapor in the sky collects in a cloud and comes down as rain.

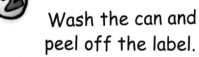